PLACE and PURPOSE

FOR PARENTS WITH TEENS

How to Bring God into the Equation

KARIN KLANCNIK

TRILOGY
A WHOLLY OWNED SUBSIDIARY OF **TBN**

PROFESSIONAL PUBLISHING MEETS POWERFUL PROMOTION

Trilogy Christian Publishers
A Wholly Owned Subsidiary of Trinity Broadcasting Network
2442 Michelle Drive
Tustin, CA 92780

For information, address Trilogy Christian Publishing
Rights Department, 2442 Michelle Drive, Tustin, CA 92780.
Trilogy Christian Publishing/ TBN and colophon are trademarks of Trinity Broadcasting Network.
For information about special discounts for bulk purchases, please contact Trilogy Christian Publishing.

10 9 8 7 6 5 4 3 2 1
Library of Congress Cataloging-in-Publication Data is available.
ISBN 979-8-89333-582-8
ISBN 979-8-89333-583-5

To all the pastors who wonder if anyone is listening…I was listening! Thank you, Robert Schuller, Phil Barnhart, Robbie DeMarigny, Eric Flood, Bill Hybels, Darren Whitehead, Burnard Scott.

Also, a big thank you to my son's mentors, Steve Williams, Josh Thomas, Ronnie Jones, Charity Hall, Gene Woods, and Steve Alvarez.

Kerrick, Gavin and Kayden, never stop searching, Love Mom.

INTRODUCTION

Before I begin to share my journey of how I found God and my life's purpose, I want to assure you that I understand that it's my journey and that your spiritual journey may be totally different. I recognize and rejoice in the basic truth that all people were created by a loving God; all people are God's special creation, and thus all people have the right to be treated with dignity and respect, regardless of their beliefs.

It is my true desire that my view of Jesus may not offend you, but enlighten you. However, if you have a hard time believing in Jesus, or you're not even sure He exists, that is your journey so far, and I completely respect that, but do me a favor and just hang on for the ride!

I assure you, this book is about a relationship, not a religion. I am not a perfect Christian. I do stupid things, I mess up, and I've gone through quite the crap, but God is still there for me! Do you know that you can talk to God and He will listen and respond?

If you and your teen are not living your best life, get ready to hear God's voice loud and clear! God's knowledge and blessings are waiting for you! It is not by chance that you are reading this. There is going to be a lot for you to think about for yourself in this book because when we can be our best selves, we can have a better influence on our children.

We all want to know: do prayers really work? Can we really pray it away or pray it so? Especially when it comes to our children. As parents, we have a beautiful universal language that we all just want our kids to be happy. When our kids become teens, there can be some really painful lessons and explosions. This is a workbook that will help you put your pain to purpose. Start aligning yourself with God's will and it will lead you into the most important relationship you will ever have. This is a book of hope and challenge that takes you through life's lessons and provides victory for living your best life!

We all long for peace and purpose, but for many of us, we don't know where to start. There is so much power in prayer, but in many cases, we don't realize this when we first start to pray. This book will help you discover how to build that relationship and start living that amazing life you were built for. So much of our teen's life depends on how we live our life, whether we want to face that or not. Our influences can take root even when we are not aware of them.

I started journaling as a desperate attempt to keep my sanity through the darkest, literally, winter I have ever had...almost fifteen years ago! I also was battling cancer and depression, and wondering *"why me? Haven't I been a faithful, good girl?"* Guess what, it's not about that!

When I discovered the secret of how to pray, how to talk to God, a vision was birthed. I actually started to believe that what I wanted could be true. When I started writing this book, I didn't know how it would end or where it would take me. I only knew I had a story to tell and hoped it would help others as the principles have helped me.

Fast forward ten years from that time, and my husband and I found ourselves unemployed and with a rebellious teen. We decided to seek professional help with Teen Challenge, and it's one of the best decisions we have ever made. It turned our family around and gave us a second chance. For those of you parents going through this also, get ready to turn things around—there is hope!

This workbook will take you on a journey of many discoveries, including: God's will, surrender, and dealing with pain. This is especially for parents of teens. If you are depressed, or know (or feel) like you are not living your best life, best marriage, or are not working in the job of your dreams; if you are in a situation where you feel there is no way out for you and your teen, that only God can fix, then get ready to see it happen. This workbook will leave you with a heart filled with thanksgiving and praise!

TABLE OF CONTENTS

CHAPTER 1:

HOW DID IT ALL START?

I am going to do the best I can to take you back to the very beginning because people often ask me, how did it get to a place where you had to send your son away? There are a few links when I think back as to how we got to where we were, and the first one was back in grade school.

My husband and I had a teacher's conference and saw our son's desk way in the back of the room, separated from the rest of the class. We were shocked because we never received an email or phone call about that. When I asked her why our son's desk was separated from the rest of the class, she said it was because he's disruptive.

Our son also did not tell us, probably because he thought he was in trouble. I couldn't believe what I was seeing and hearing because at that age, kids are just trying to fit in and I'm sure he felt ostracized. This carried through middle school and my son continued to feel alone. He had a few friends but not strong enough connections to make him feel safe or loved.

When he reached high school, he started to get into trouble. He would sneak out and we would get phone calls from the police in the middle of the night. He was so desperate for friends and to fit in that I believe he would have done just about anything. His grades were failing, despite being extremely intelligent. About this time, we found out our son was bullied and made fun of in front of his math class by his teacher. The school officials actually suggested we pull him from school, so we did. He tried some online classes, but his loneliness only intensified.

We decided to move and have him start fresh in a new school. It was very hard to get our son involved in healthy activities because he was very good at sports that were not part of school, such as water and snow skiing. Things got ugly very quickly. He made friends with a few other troublemakers and things escalated.

We were monitoring his phone and as soon as we saw the word "*gun*," we knew we had to get professional help. I felt God pressing on my heart to enroll him at Teen Challenge Adventure Ranch. I thought maybe they could connect with him through his outdoorsy adventurous side. I was right. It was quite a year. We actually had to sign our parental rights over to them that year, which was one of the scariest things we ever had to do. However, I do believe our son would not be alive today if it weren't for

Teen Challenge.

Of course, there were a lot of things that we could have done better as parents, and that is my hope for writing this book and telling my story. So perhaps you can see the signs early, and your journey may not be as painful as ours.

Teens have to deal with so much stress these days. As parents there are things we can and should do, and things we shouldn't do. I pray that we can start supporting each other as parents instead of judging one another. In the following chapters, I write about things we humbly learned from Teen Challenge when going through their program as parents, *not from doing all these things correctly*! There are many things I wish we could get a second chance at and do over, but I see the blessing that my son is alive and thriving, and that's all that really matters. Praise God!

CHAPTER 2:

COMMUNITY

The rebellion of children against their parents is hitting an all-time high. As parents we could all have good intentions, but we just don't know what is going on. There is too much of a secret community on the internet that teens share, and often it can be very dark. I remember hearing about the dark web for the first time. I was so scared that there was even such a thing out there so easily accessible for teens! I was scared as to how long my boys may have known about it before I did. It's a world that can happen behind our backs and grab our children and pull them in.

There is a chance that as parents we will continue to be in the darkness as to what to do unless we *"put on the full armor of God"* (Ephesians 6:11). God also says in Ephesians 6 that our struggles are not of this world but are against the spiritual forces of evil. Unless we take our stand with faith, we may not be able to *"extinguish all the flaming arrows of the evil one."*

In Hosea 4:6 it says, "My people are destroyed from lack of knowledge. Because you have rejected knowledge, I also reject you as my priests; because you have ignored the law of your God; I also will ignore your children." I don't know about you, but that is scary knowledge right there.

Later, there is a chapter on phone and computer use, but in this chapter, I want you to concentrate on the teen's community and what it looks like. I start the second chapter with this because if we could have gotten at least this in place, it may not have gotten so bad. Does your child have a community of friends, coaches, parents, and teachers that know what is going on in their lives? If not, this will be a big part of your homework.

Our relationships should manifest where we come from, morally and ethically, and reflect the nature of God. Our relationships with our teens should:

1. Encourage them.

2. Support them emotionally.

3. Challenge them to think.

4. Tell them the truth in love.

We were created for relationships, and Jesus came to restore our relationships. Within this we must concede our need for others (1 Corinthians 12:20–26.) Relationships balance our needs and increase our strength. Here are relationships that our teens may be involved in and need to avoid:

1. Teens who can't control their anger

2. Teens who lie

3. Teens who like to argue

4. Teens who gossip

5. Teens who steal or do drugs (this one may be obvious, but I need to mention it)

*If our teens have relationships with others who are living in darkness, how can they not be in the darkness? Proverbs 13:20 says, *"Walk with the wise and become wise, for a companion of fools suffers harm."*

Our teens need friends more than ever at this age, but if they are friends who are leading them into darkness, they may need to start over with better friends. This will be a tough task and may require some drastic changes. Right now, take this time to be honest and evaluate your child's community or lack of one.

1.) Evaluate your child's friends. First, make a list of all your child's friends. Put them into a category of A, B or C friends. A—a great friend with good character and influence. B—a good friend but may need more supervision. C—not good for my child at all.

_____

_____

_____

_____

_____

_____

_____

2.) Make a list of those friends' parents and their phone numbers:

_____

_____

_____

_____

_____

_____

_____

3.) Does your child have a teacher or a coach that you trust for time and advice?

_____

_____

_____

_____

_____

_____

_____

4.) Does your child have a mentor? (An adult outside of family that can take a special positive interest in your child.)

_____

_____

_____

_____

_____

_____

5.) Does your child know a pastor or youth pastor?

_____

_____

_____

_____

_____

_____

6.) Does your child have a trusted aunt or uncle to turn to for advice or just to talk to?

_____

_____

_____

_____

_____

_____

_____

7.) What is your conclusion regarding your child's community in general?

_____

_____

_____

_____

_____

_____

*There are things that we will need to do or not do to get them to this goal. Here are some things we need to sacrifice as parents to get them to their goal. Again, you will need to humble yourselves and be as honest with yourself as possible.

1.) You must not have your emotional needs met through your child.

_____

_____

_____

_____

_____

_____

2.) Time and energy will need to be sacrificed. (This will be extremely difficult for traveling or physically distant jobs.)

_____

_____

_____

_____

_____

_____

3.) Avoid focusing on gaining popularity with your child. (Reflect on what this means to you.)

_____

_____

_____

_____

_____

_____

_____

4.) Don't look to your child for validation.

_____

_____

_____

_____

_____

_____

_____

Dear Lord, thank You for giving us incredible power and authority over our children. Help us to administer this authority in Your name. Help us to use this power for Your purposes. When Jesus lived on earth, He took care of "the least of them." Help us to live by Your example. You love to see us come together and be united in honor of Your name. I so want to be a part of that. Help us to use the talents You have given us to accomplish this and influence our greatest gifts...our children. "How good and pleasant it is when brothers live together in unity!" (Psalm 133:1).

CHAPTER 3:

REFLECTION IS NECESSARY

Sometimes the need to feel sorry for ourselves is so strong, especially when no one else does. We reason, *"Maybe if I wallow in my pity, God will eventually feel so sorry for me that He will change my circumstances."* How wrong that is! As a matter of fact, God despises self-pity and prayers will never be answered in this state of mind. We can't help our teens until we help ourselves. When we reflect or meditate on God's Word, His saving grace, and His answered prayers, that's when we will eventually see the light and have revelation! God is looking to help heal the family as a unit.

God wants to hear our sorrows, but to reflect constantly on them is another story. This shows a lack of trust and a wavering faith. God wants a relationship with us, not just for us to know His basic truth. It takes two-way communication with Him, just as we do with our best human friend. Prayer is our way to communicate with God, but meditation and reflection is His way to communicate with us! If we are too busy blabbing away or too busy in general, we will miss what God wants to say to us. Even in our most dire circumstances, we need to learn that, through faith, God will work out all things for good. So it is extremely important *what* we reflect on.

Have you ever wondered what God wants to tell you? This is your chance: take some time to reflect on everything that has gone right in your life. Reflect and see how God has had a hand in all of it. Reflect on His Word and what He wants to tell you. Reflection is not a time to sit quietly and let your mind wander. Reflection takes controlled and focused thinking on God and His greatness, not on you. There are many ways we can worship and feel close to God. Find what works best for you.

When we can live in gratitude through reflection, we will give a gift to our children. Modeling this behavior and practice is crucial. I love nature, so reflecting in an outdoor setting works well for me. Make your relationship with God unique, just as He designed you to be. Here are some questions to ponder. I encourage you to print and give your child the following sheet for them to fill out as well.

QUESTIONS FOR REFLECTION AND PERSONAL WORK

1.) I was the happiest during this time or this year in my life....

_____

_____

_____

_____

_____

_____

_____

2.) I was happy because....

_____

_____

_____

_____

_____

_____

_____

3.) I am praying about....

_____

_____

_____

_____

_____

_____

_____

4.) I don't think God will answer because....

_____

_____

_____

_____

_____

5.) I do think God will answer because....

_____

_____

_____

_____

_____

6.) This is something that I think could be getting in the way of my relationship with God....

_____

_____

_____

_____

_____

_____

_____

7.) I feel the closest to God when....

_____

_____

_____

_____

_____

8.) This is the time of day I will set aside to be quiet and listen to God....

_____

_____

_____

_____

_____

_____

9.) I commit to growing my relationship with God. (Sign your name.)

_____

_____

_____

_____

_____

_____

_____

Dear Lord, thank You for the people reading this today. We both know that this is no accident for them to be reading this. You so desire for us to discover what Your will is for us. You want a relationship with us and our children. Thank You that with your help we can start that today. "Therefore, if anyone is in Christ, the new creation has come: The old has gone, the new is here!" (2 Corinthians 5:17.) Thank You for our children, and all that they can teach us. We may have more experience and wisdom than they do, but their wonderment and innocence might be exactly what we need to have to have a new perspective on life.

Help us to invest in our children's future. Help us to not always focus on what we can give our children physically but how we can help them emotionally and steer them to You! Help us to show what Christ did for us and God's amazing love He has for them. Thank you for telling us..."Truly I tell you, unless you change and become like little children, you will never enter the kingdom of heaven" (Matthew 18:3–4).

CHAPTER 4:

LIFE-CONTROLLING ISSUES

Today's life-controlling issues seem bigger, scarier, and more prominent. Think about it, when I was young, there was alcohol or marijuana. Now we have scary things like opioids and fentanyl. I personally have a very good friend who has lost his only two sons to fentanyl. I have cried many tears for him. Years ago, a teen could have bought a Playboy magazine; now we have graphic pornography with the click of a button. I can remember my son in sixth grade did not have a phone yet, so a friend in school told him to go home on the computer and click on, *"Want to have some fun."* It turned out to be a porn site. We had the computer in the kitchen, so you can imagine to all our surprise what we saw.

Imagine now with kids having smart phones in grade school what is available to them. I would suggest looking into as many monitoring and blocking apps as you can find. There are more and more parental services for phones these days, so please do your research.

There are so many things that can take unhealthy control of our lives. Drugs, alcohol, gambling, pornography, overeating, compulsive spending, video games, pain pills, and even watching TV. In 1 Corinthians 6:12, we are told *"not to be mastered by anything."* When we have a controlling life issue, we start to see a distorted reality, and often push people away who really care about us the most.

In a future chapter, I will mention how quiet kids, at times, can be the most dangerous situation. It's time as a parent to play detective. Privacy should no longer be honored when we think our child's life is in danger. If you feel your child is in danger of taking his/her own life, or someone else's life, please get help immediately. Do not wait another minute.

One Sunday our son thought we were on our way to church, but instead we ended up that day driving him all the way to Arkansas from Wisconsin for rehabilitation. There is no need to pack or prepare when your child's life is in danger, just action!

When we or our children are dominated by an overpowering influence, we need to do all we can to point them into the freedom of living with Christ. This is the only thing that will give physical, emotional, and spiritual freedom. Romans 6:14 says, *"For sin shall no longer be your master, because you are not under the law, but under grace.*" These life-controlling issues do not happen overnight; no one plans for them so we must identify a possible problem immediately. Unfortunately, just taking our teens to church will not be enough. Do not avoid such matters because of shame or embarrassment. These issues happen to the best of parents and the best of kids! We need to be open to the Lord working in our lives before problems take root. Ignoring such issues does not make them go away!

Dear Lord, I know it breaks Your heart when You see Your children, old and young, living under the control of substances; for some, it's a lifetime of control. We ask that You break those chains. We want to make You proud, Father. We want to live in freedom. Give us the resources and bring people into our lives to help. Thank You for Your forgiveness and Your open arms waiting for us. You are such a good, good, Father. Amen!

QUESTIONS FOR REFLECTION AND PERSONAL WORK

1.) Do I have a life-controlling issue that I need to recognize?

_____

_____

_____

_____

_____

_____

_____

2.) Is my behavior done in secret?

_____

_____

_____

_____

_____

_____

3.) Do my life-controlling issues affect the ones I love?

_____

_____

_____

_____

_____

_____

_____

4.) Does my behavior reflect Christ's love?

_____

_____

_____

_____

_____

5.) Do I do certain things to escape my reality?

_____

_____

_____

_____

_____

6.) Do I feel I have a good monitoring system for my child?

_____

_____

_____

_____

_____

_____

_____

7.) Do I downplay possible red flags from my child?

_____

_____

_____

_____

_____

_____

_____

CHAPTER 5:

ISOLATION

The perception of what we see on social media, especially what teens see, is that people are happy, successful, have lots of friends, are talented, beautiful, and have it all together. The reality is that sometimes the more people boast on their social media, the more they are looking for validation and admiration and in reality, can be quite lonely. I'm sure as parents you have felt hurt over social media—imagine how our teens feel when their brains and bodies are still developing!

Many teens will withdraw and isolate because they feel they are not good enough for the people that are putting on such a strong, confident image. Most teens suffer from a strong inferiority complex. Teens can be blind to their own feelings, and desperation for acceptance can take over. When this happens, they can often experiment with dangerous behavior just to get noticed or feel accepted.

Not only will some teens isolate themselves from others, but they can isolate themselves from God. When this happens, they can feel a level of loneliness that is unbearable and turn to anything that will take that loneliness away. If their relationship with God is strong, time alone with God will not only feel good, but will be necessary. Being aware and understanding that not everything is what it seems can really help us and our children make healthy choices.

We don't have to be jealous, or sad, or envious of what we see, if we know that's not what reality is. Staying in check with our emotions can help us feel content and secure. We can also take care of hidden emotions, such as anger and fear, before they get the best of us. *"God sets the lonely in families, he leads forth the prisoners with singing"* (Psalm 68:6).

Dear Lord, we have created an atmosphere around us that creates much loneliness and isolation, and I know that was not Your plan. Forgive us and help us to live lives that You intended with peace and purpose. Help us to help the younger generation to be aware of those around them that may need their spirits lifted. Thank You that You are always there when we need someone. You are the best friend we could ever have. I pray for those reading this to have a newfound relationship with You. Amen.

QUESTIONS FOR REFLECTION AND PERSONAL WORK

1.) Does my teen talk about their feelings easily?

_____

_____

_____

_____

_____

_____

2.) What can I do to help healthy relationships flourish?

_____

_____

_____

_____

_____

3.) Do I model healthy friendships for my child?

_____

_____

_____

_____
_____
_____
_____

4.) Does my child spend a significant time alone?

_____
_____
_____
_____
_____
_____

5.) Do I have a quiet time I can spend with God?

_____
_____
_____
_____
_____
_____

CHAPTER 6:

WHAT IS THE LESSON?

Just like life is a test, life should be a lesson. We should never feel we have learned everything. As soon as we stop learning, pride enters in. In every situation and life experience, we have an opportunity to learn something. Even if we have learned the lesson before, sometimes we need a reminder. God loves it when we can learn from each other. If we try to do everything ourselves and not practice faith, we are not teachable, and our sufferings will be wasted and worthless. God will not be able to use us if we are not teachable.

Victorious living, free from depression or anxiety, will require obedience to the Lord and a teachable attitude. It takes a lot of work, but the freedom and peace are worth it! It takes evaluating your physical needs, disciplining your mind, learning your spiritual needs, and committing to all of these things. In the same way that you must put your oxygen mask on first before assisting your child on an airplane, I'm going to ask you to do the same with this workbook. There will be a separate workbook for teens, but through these chapters, let's try to concentrate on ourselves.

Remember, the truth is light, and only the truth will set us free. We can experience glorious freedom from any depression, addiction, or struggle we have that we are being held bondage to, but we must ask God to show us the truth if we don't see it. Decide now and ask God to reveal these things to you.

Dear Lord, I ask that the lessons that are learned continue to surprise us. Sometimes we know what to do, but we don't do it anyway. Keep us in the truth so we can stay spiritually strong. I ask for more outdoor time, balanced nutrition, adequate sleep, and to open our eyes to all the other things that can influence mental health. Thank You that we can start new today and everything else is in the past. I pray for everyone who is reading this to learn their life lessons. I understand, Lord, that You have called us, and it is our responsibility to answer that call.... "For many are invited, but few are chosen" (Matthew 22:14).

QUESTIONS FOR REFLECTION AND PERSONAL WORK

1.) What are some things that I think may lead me to feel sad, anxious, or depressed?

_____

_____

_____

_____

_____

_____

2.) What are things that I can change in my life that may help me?

_____

_____

_____

_____

_____

3.) What are some life lessons I have had?

_____

_____

_____

_____

_____

_____

_____

4.) Who can I share with that might benefit from hearing my struggles?

_____

_____

_____

_____

5.) Do I really believe I can surrender this to God? Why or why not?

_____

_____

_____

_____

_____

6.) Am I emotionally available to my child/ spouse/ friends?

_____

_____

_____

_____

_____

_____

_____

CHAPTER 7:

BLESSED AND DEPRESSED

If you've ever been depressed, know of someone that suffers from depression, or perhaps find yourself wondering how anyone could possibly be depressed, then this book is for you. For most people it's just a short season, but if not recognized or dealt with, it can go on for years, even decades! You know what I have learned through all this? Well, I've learned a lot, but one thing that's true is, you can tell people you have cancer, or any other sickness for that matter, such as drug or alcohol addiction, even pornography addiction, and they will pray for you, and try to help you in any way they can.

However, as soon as you tell them you are depressed, they don't know what to do; especially if you have a fairly blessed or abundant life. They look at you as an ungrateful person who has been blessed but doesn't see his/her blessings. Imagine how hard it must be for our kids to recognize this and then admit to it. Our mental health is struggling, and we must help one another.

Unfortunately, people usually see depression as only a mental problem and not a physical or spiritual problem. I can tell you right now, it is a problem for all three. I am not a doctor or a pastor, but seeing my roller coaster of personality during the winter and summer has made me very aware of the reality of SAD (Seasonal Affective Disorder). That's why I now live in southern Florida! Now, before you decide, *"That's it, we just need to move,"* that's only part of it. Where we live makes a huge difference in our mojo and our purpose, but packing up and moving will only be a temporary fix, so stick with me and dig in and do the work!

How can you expect to read a book and be ready to conquer anything that comes your way? Heal your marriage, heal your relationship with your teen, get out of the pit of depression, break the chains of life-controlling issues. If you are willing to put in the work, I believe you can help yourself and your child.

QUESTIONS FOR REFLECTION AND PERSONAL WORK

1.) Would it help me or my teen to move?

_____

_____

_____

_____

_____

_____

_____

2.) Am I living in a city due to a marriage? Do I like it there?

_____

_____

_____

_____

_____

_____

_____

3.) Would my spouse be open to moving? How could I approach him or her on this matter?

_____

_____

_____

_____

_____

_____

_____

4.) Am I feeling stuck in a particular city due to a job or financial situation?

_____

_____

_____

_____

_____

_____

5.) If I could live anywhere I want, what would be the first place that comes to mind?

_____

_____

_____

_____

_____

_____

Dear Lord, I pray for this person who desires to move. It can feel like such a big task. There are jobs to think about, often homes to sell, marriages and kids to think about. Nothing is too great or too big for You, Lord. Give this person a vision of how this can work. Help them to think of the bigger picture and not let all the details weigh them down.

If this person feels they are living in the perfect spot, Lord, give them a new appreciation of where they are. Help them to feel grateful and to know that You are always at work. Even when we are not aware of it, You are working for our good! Amen to Your power! Give this person the strength to continue this journey of self-discovery and understand that this is just some of the rough edges being chipped away.

CHAPTER 8:

DEVASTATION IS UNPREDICTABLE

I can remember shortly after we moved to California when I was sixteen, I started to adjust and feel at peace. My parents were getting along great and my dad was sober. I felt like my problems were in the past and God had saved my life in many ways. Then I got a dreadful phone call. I was told that my best friend throughout my childhood in Wisconsin had drowned. All the days of swimming, playing red-light green-light and tag, selling worms and lemonade, family ski trips up north, and hanging out at the firepit flashed before my eyes.

Oh man, every time I think of it, I get sick! It still stings thirty-seven years later. My memories of our time back in Wisconsin were being ripped from my heart. I felt guilty for not being there. I threw myself on the floor and sobbed and sobbed. He was an expert swimmer! It was just a freak accident while he was putting in a raft. I screamed to God, *"Why?"* I still often wonder why God saved me and not him.

This story shows that you never know what life will throw at you. I'm sure many of you have found this out from COVID, and have lost loved ones. For that, I am so very sorry. You can think you are out of tough times and then something new can hit you. That is why we must live life to the fullest at all times. Life is unpredictable, and so are hard times.

Only God knows the mysteries of life, such as why children and babies die. How do we go on when such things happen? You may be asking, *"Don't we deserve to be depressed when such tragedy comes our way?"* Well, we deserve to feel however we feel, but for how long? Would one month be long enough to grieve? One year?

Sometimes the pain will last a lifetime, but we can either find a way to enjoy life, or we can waste our life being depressed forever, missing out on all God has in store for us, and it's more than we can imagine! I guess I decided that's not what my friend Jon would have wanted. God doesn't want that either. Jon would have wanted his family and me to really live, as he very much did.

God wants us to cry out to Him so He can deliver us from our pain and depression because those things sadden Him. If we never experience pain and never receive God's love, then He can never receive the glory for helping and delivering us. Only God's power in these situations can bring us the hope we need.

Sometimes when I look at other people's sufferings, I feel like I have it so easy. I guess if we look hard enough, there will always be someone who seems to have it worse than we do. Sometimes there are certain kinds of suffering that just seem more painful or unsolvable than others. I know time can't mend all things, but it sure can help us manage our pain.

Dear Lord, thank You that you hear us when we cry out to You. You care and love us much more than a human father or mother loves their son and daughter. You know every hair that is on our heads, and You care about every concern we have. Your power and plans are so great; I can't possibly wrap my little brain around it. Thank You for Jon. Thank You for the person reading this. Thank You for the years they had with their special loved ones, no matter how brief or long it was. Thank You that if they put their faith in You, they will see their loved ones again someday. Thank You for giving us that hope.

> *"He will wipe every tear from their eyes. There will be no more death or mourning or crying or pain, for the old order of things has passed away" (Revelation 21:4).*

This is a sensitive subject. Take some time to reflect and grieve as necessary. Then pick yourself back up. We are only allowed to grieve for a few days, not weeks. Trust me, this discipline will help.

59

QUESTIONS FOR REFLECTION AND PERSONAL WORK

1.) Who have I lost that I or my child may not have grieved properly?

_____

_____

_____

_____

_____

_____

_____

2.) Is it possible that there may be a lesson in such a loss? What may this be?

_____

_____

_____

_____

_____

_____

_____

3.) Would this person want me to be happy right now and live the best life I can?

_____

_____

_____

_____

_____

_____

4.) How can I make this person proud or pass on a legacy if possible?

_____

_____

_____

_____

_____

_____

5.) For teens: do you miss a friend? Write a letter to that friend about how you feel, even if you will never see them again, or even if they have passed away. (No one has to read this if you choose. But if it will help you to communicate how you are feeling, I suggest letting one or both of your parents read it.)

_____

_____

_____

_____

_____

_____

_____

CHAPTER 9:

HELPING OTHERS

We all know the fact that we always feel better about ourselves when we can help others. I think people underestimate the importance and impact it can have on children and teens. This is where some serious breakthrough can happen. Even if it's just for a day, or even an hour, commit yourself and your teen to plan on something you can do for others.

It may be to babysit for a neighbor, cook a meal for a local pantry, or for an elderly neighbor. Perhaps even cleaning a church's bathroom. This activity done together can be a great bonding experience. If your teen is reluctant, plan something on your own and tell them you need their help.

There are many things we can do to help; we just have to do them. You will feel good about helping others and see that the true blessing will fall upon you. When you start taking the focus off of yourself, your mental health will be at its best, but most of all, when you stop concentrating on your own needs, you will become more aware of the needs around you.

When doing such things, along with praying diligently, one can often discover their life's mission or purpose. When this happens, you can see yourself pouring your most tragic circumstances into helping others in the same situation. Your deepest hurts and sufferings will become a lamppost to those in the dark. There is nothing more exciting than this! There are many young adults who discover their purpose by helping others in the same stressful situation they have been under.

Dear Lord, thank You for revealing to me my life purpose. Please reveal the same to those who are reading this. Bring parents and teens together in a deep way with a simple meal or act of kindness. We will continue to trust You and never doubt that any of this is a waste of time or effort (1 Corinthians 15:58). I pray that we continue to keep our focus on helping others and not on ourselves. Thank You that Your gifts are amazing and keep us in awe of You. Thank You, that when everything else fails in this world, we have You to lean on. Thank you that You are making us strong in our weakness. You have said, "My grace is sufficient for you, for my power is made perfect in weakness" (2 Corinthians 12:9).

QUESTIONS FOR REFLECTION AND PERSONAL WORK

1.) I am committing myself to volunteer to help a person or organization in the following week.

_____

_____

_____

_____

_____

_____

_____

Sign here: _____

2.) I will commit to doing this whether I can get my teen to come or not, and I will share my experience with him/her.

_____

_____

_____

_____

_____

_____

_____

3.) I think my teen would enjoy helping someone in this capacity:

_____

_____

_____

_____

_____

_____

4.) I will make this a high priority no matter what other commitments we have.

_____

_____

_____

_____

_____

_____

_____

Sign here: _____

5.) I will commit to doing such an activity with my teen for at least a month before I give up.

_____

_____

_____

_____

_____

_____

_____

6.) I will start calling local churches or organizations right now to see where help is needed.

_____

_____

_____

_____

_____

_____

_____

CHAPTER 10:

HOW DO WE REACT TO AN ATTACK?

Our response to someone's attack can tell us a lot about our emotional intelligence. My mentor, who has her masters in emotional intelligence education, has always told me, *"Someone with a high EQ will be much more successful in life than a person with a high IQ."* I don't think she was downplaying the fact that it is important to be book smart, just more the fact that life can throw so many more things at us that need a high EQ (emotional intelligence).

It is really hard to react to an attack properly when we are down or frustrated, but that is when we need to take a step back and pause. Pause for as long as we need to control our feelings. We mustn't let attacks have more power than they deserve.

One thing that we have to get very clear is that our teens need our respect first, regardless of whether they give it to us. I am always amazed at how many teachers do not grasp this concept. When it comes to parent-teen relationships, our teens will often surprise us with respect when respect is given, but very rarely do they know how to give it first. It is possible to be direct and frank, but kind. "All you need to say is simply 'Yes' or 'No'; anything beyond this comes from the evil one" (Matthew 5:37). Here are some key components of conflict you will need to practice with your teen.

1.) Guide your child to deal with his/her anger.

2.) Take a break...pause often.

3.) Acknowledge his/her distress.

4.) Lower your voice, over and over again.

5.) Be calm!

6.) Communicate your alliance (you are fighting for your son/daughter).

_____

_____

_____

_____

_____

_____

_____

7.) Again, communicate respect, regardless of if it is returned.

_____

_____

_____

_____

_____

_____

Allowing ourselves to be offended by our child keeps us from parenting effectively. Anger will always look for a target. Remember, there will be conflict, but you can't control anyone but yourself! (See Proverbs 19:1–3.) Our spiritual awareness and emotional intelligence will contain a great deal of self-control, and the Bible has a great deal to say on the subject.

Self-control involves a great deal of effort...it's hard work! Many teens live with hidden anxiety, anger, and fear. Most of the time there is no baseline for this, but not dealing with these emotions has only exasperated them. So, there they sit and it can come out at any time and for very little reason. When they become aware of these emotions they harbor, they are on their way to the emotional intelligence I spoke of. They can recognize when these feelings are surfacing and deal with them head-on before they become out of control or attack someone.

Unhealthy emotions bottled up or kept hidden can lead to relapses in recovery from addictions and dependencies. Fear and anger are some of the most difficult feelings to express. If not dealt with, they can lead to more isolation.

Dear Lord, we ask You now to reveal any hidden fear or anger we may have bottled up inside. We know that when we do not deal with our true feelings or what is really bothering us, our problems usually just get worse. Help us to be open, honest, and vulnerable to others so a breakthrough can happen. Help us to be sensitive to how we react to an attack and stay calm.

God, we know You love it when we can learn from each other, so we ask You now to show us the truth. Whatever the kind of experience that has led us to fear and anger can finally be broken with your power. You are the only one that can help us overcome such feelings. "Losing your temper causes a lot of trouble, but staying calm settles arguments" (Proverbs 15:18, CEV).

QUESTIONS FOR REFLECTION AND PERSONAL WORK

1.) What is a part of my life I enjoy? What is a part that is difficult for me?

_____

_____

_____

_____

_____

_____

2.) What is something that makes me lose my temper? What is something that makes my teen lose his or her temper?

_____

_____

_____

_____

_____

_____

3.) Have I ever told someone of a controlling emotion I have? If not, am I willing to do so?

_____

_____

_____

_____

_____

4.) Am I willing to surrender my anger and fears to God? If I could, how could this change how I feel about things?

_____

_____

_____

_____

_____

5.) Pray to God and let Him know your inner fears and anger. Ask Him to have power and authority over these emotions.

_____

_____

_____

_____

_____

_____

_____

CHAPTER 11:

IDENTIFY PHYSICAL NEEDS

You can't begin your healing or hear God's voice as clearly if you don't take care of your physical needs first. I am not a physician, but I know there are several elements to healing. Physical needs are just as important as our emotional and spiritual needs. Researching this has really helped me identify some things that may have contributed to my healing. This was a big step in coming out of my depression, as I was in some serious need of supplements, exercise, and hormones. I'm sure in some cases an antidepressant is necessary. Please continue to seek medical or psychological care. This book is not a substitute but an addition to your care.

A person may be lacking needed exercise, sun, or certain vitamins. Unfortunately, when you're depressed, it's even harder to get motivated to exercise. This will be a challenge but will be necessary if you want to live your best life. Having a dog is always a good excuse to go out for a walk. Would this be a consideration for your family?

The next need to recognize is nutritional balance. More and more studies are linking malnutrition to depression and even cancer. There may be an imbalance in your teen's hormones, thus causing mood swings! They could be on the wrong dose of supplements, or wrong supplements altogether, which could have devastating physical and emotional effects. You could be the happiest person on this planet, but it could be only a matter of time until a nutritional imbalance starts affecting you emotionally. It's always important to check with your doctor on supplements. It is my personal opinion that we are destroying our lives by all the sugar intake we have—darn! I love sugar!

The last is spiritual connection. If we are not connected in some way to the spiritual health our souls desire, we will always feel unfulfilled and empty. There is nothing else that can fill that void, no matter how we try. No relationship, job, or millions of dollars can fill this void; not even a move to the beach! Our souls and bodies were designed for that spiritual connection. Generally, people who are depressed will be deficient in one or more of these physical, emotional, or spiritual needs, and sometimes it's all of them.

Dear Lord, You made us to live abundantly. Help us to not get in our own way! We want to eat healthy, but our willpower is weak. We want to have a close marriage and good friends, but sometimes we tend to blame problems on them and not look at ourselves. We want to exercise, but we're so tired! Give us the energy, Lord. We need to do what You designed us to do, that is....to shine bright! Thank You for that. We need to "watch and pray so that [we] will not fall into temptation. The spirit is willing, but the body is weak" (Matthew 26:41).

QUESTIONS FOR REFLECTION AND PERSONAL WORK

1.) Am I or my teen in the best physical shape we can be in? What do I need to do to make that happen? What is my first step in the right direction?

_____

_____

_____

_____

_____

_____

_____

2.) Are they on any supplements? How can I implement that into our daily routine?

_____

_____

_____

_____

_____

_____

_____

3.) Are we eating a well-balanced diet? Do I believe that would make a difference? If I don't, we may never eat to provide for our health.

_____

_____

_____

_____

_____

_____

_____

4.) Do I feel spiritually connected? Is my child in a relationship with the Lord? Do I honestly feel that this will make a difference in my job? Marriage? Teens? If the answer is no, hang on for the ride!

_____

_____

_____

_____

_____

_____

_____

5.) Do I value my body as a holy temple?

_____

_____

_____

_____

_____

_____

_____

CHAPTER 12:

FORGIVENESS AND FREEDOM

We often don't recognize the unforgiveness that is in us. We must pray about this and ask God to reveal this in our hearts. Whoever does not forgive ultimately grows hate in their heart. We must forgive, no matter how that person makes us feel. It is a decision we make regardless of our circumstances. If we wait until that person makes us feel good, or says they are sorry, we could wait a lifetime.

Ultimately, the consequences for our unforgiveness fall on us. We make ourselves depressed because the lack of forgiveness is harbored in our hearts and makes us sick. Jesus felt so strongly on this matter that He said, *"Anyone who hates a brother or sister is a murderer, and you know that no murderer has eternal life residing in him"* (1 John 3:15).

We often hear people say, well, I don't hate that person and I forgive them, I just don't like them. You can fool yourself, but there is no fooling God. He knows what is in our hearts and what we don't speak of. *"Be kind and compassionate to one another, forgiving each other, just as in Christ, God forgave you"* (Ephesians 4:32).

Forgiveness is such a hard thing when people have really wronged us. How can we ever get to the point of forgiveness? Pray! Pray every day on the matter and God will give you the strength to let it go—finally! Jesus gave us a very challenging commandment. Imagine if we could really live this out?

> *You have heard that it was said, 'Eye for eye, and tooth for tooth.' But I tell you, do not resist an evil person. If anyone slaps you on the right cheek, turn to them the other cheek also. And if anyone wants to sue you and take your shirt, hand over your coat as well. If anyone forces you to go one mile, go with them two miles. Give to the one who asks you, and do not turn away from the one who wants to borrow from you.*
>
> **Matthew 5:38–42**

QUESTIONS FOR REFLECTION AND PERSONAL WORK

1.) Towards whom have I been harboring resentment? Would it make a difference in my life or my child's life if I were able to forgive that person or persons? Is your child not willing to forgive someone?

_____

_____

_____

_____

_____

_____

2.) Who have I wronged that may need a simple apology from me? How would I feel doing that? What would my child think?

_____

_____

_____

_____

_____

_____

3.) True or False: I feel that I may not be living a blessed life because I have resentment in my life.

_____

_____

_____

_____

_____

_____

4.) True or False: The people I have ill feelings toward deserve my wrath.

_____

_____

_____

_____

_____

_____

5.) Has it been long enough? Could now be the time in my life to extend peace?

_____

_____

_____

_____

_____

_____

_____

6.) True or False: Do I really believe I can do all things through Christ who strengthens me?

_____

_____

_____

_____

_____

_____

7.) Along with your child, write down how someone has wronged them and without letting anyone else read it, find a firepit and burn it.

_____

_____

_____

_____

_____

_____

Dear Lord, I pray for those who have unforgiveness in their hearts. Thank You for revealing this in my own heart. Thank You that I can surrender all of this to You, and You can give me the peace that comes with forgiveness. Thank You for not only opening my heart but opening my eyes to the suffering around me.

I pray that You will reach those who are in such despair, and when they see no way out, Lord, show them the way. Open their eyes so they can feel the peace they so much deserve. Help us to heal our relationships, even if it is only for our child's sake. Perhaps we need to hold our tongue. Help us to do that in the future. "Sin is not ended by multiplying words, but the prudent hold their tongues" (Proverbs 10:19).

CHAPTER 13:

PASS NO JUDGMENT

One of my dearest friends is Jewish. I have been able to witness the alienation and judgment she has had to endure living in a predominantly Christian community. I also have a best friend since high school who is gay. Both of these lovely humans love their God as they understand Him. Who would I be to judge how they love their God? Of course, I desire for them to know Christ as I do, but that is in God's timing.

If we are to live our best life through Christ, then let's concentrate on getting healthy ourselves and not do what society is trying to tell us. We may feel we are not even worthy of God's love because of our past or current lifestyle. Sorry, but that's baloney! If you cut God out of your life because you feel it's an all or nothing, then you will miss out on the most amazing life God has in store for you.

I was fortunate to be able to attend my friend's son's *bar mitzvah*. I loved how she described the feeling she had when she saw all of her friends and family arm in arm dancing in a circle, not knowing who was Jewish and who wasn't. I didn't realize, but I was arm in arm with her brother, who I didn't know, and who was Jewish, and my husband was arm in arm with her college roommate, who he didn't know, and who was a strict Catholic. It just didn't matter. We were there to celebrate her son, and it didn't matter whether we celebrate the same traditions or not. It was a circle of celebration, with different beliefs, and it was beautiful.

I've seen stay-at-home moms judge working moms and working moms judge stay-at-home moms. Aren't all moms just trying to do the best we can in our circumstances? I have also seen women trying to get pregnant and judge women who already had children and yet were depressed because they couldn't get pregnant again. *"She already has two kids. What is she so sad about?"*

Judging each other puts a barrier between women who each need all the support they can get! The minute we put judgment on someone, that same circumstance can come our way. I've seen it happen time and time again. Just look at what America has turned into with our political parties, each judging the other for their beliefs.

QUESTIONS FOR REFLECTION AND PERSONAL WORK

1.) Who have I been judging, and is that judging getting in the way of living my best life for success?

_____

_____

_____

_____

_____

_____

_____

2.) Are there some opinions of mine that might be racist or judgmental?

_____

_____

_____

_____

_____

_____

_____

3.) Are there areas in my life that I may need to soften (political) or strengthen (standing up for the underprivileged)?

_____

_____

_____

_____

_____

_____

_____

4.) How could this change my life if I were more compassionate for people that don't have the same beliefs as me?

_____

_____

_____

_____

_____

_____

5.) True or False: I model *"no judgment"* behavior to my child.

_____

_____

_____

_____

_____

_____

_____

6.) True or False: It seems people of a certain type have it all together? How would my point of view change if I knew that wasn't true?

_____

_____

_____

_____

_____

_____

_____

7.) True or False: I have a hard time trusting *"the church,"* because I have gotten burned in the past. If you answered True, write down your experience in 2–3 pages, find a firepit, and watch the paper burn.

_____

_____

_____

_____

_____

Dear Lord, help us not to judge people. You are the ultimate judge, not us. Help us to love and respect all people of all backgrounds, of all different faiths, different races, and different educational backgrounds, and mostly, those who are suffering with loss and pain. Until I walk in someone's shoes, I may never know what it's like to not be able to have a child, or to lose a child, or to have a physical handicap, or to go through a divorce, or to be a single parent.

Help me, Lord, to have compassion for them all. Thank You for teaching us: "Do not judge or you too will be judged. For in the same way, you judge others, you will be judged, and with the measure you use, it will be measured to you" (Matthew 7:1–2).

CHAPTER 14:

BURNED BY THE CHURCH OR RELIGION

We *all* come from such different upbringings and backgrounds. Some of us were raised in a strict religious home and others may have never gone to church at all. Some of our interactions with the church or with Christians may have put a sour taste in our mouth. Some of us have even felt burned by the church in one way or another.

Can I be the first one to say how very sorry I am? Unfortunately, people in church and even pastors are still only human and will sin and let us down. We are not to hold our hope in a pastor or a particular church. They are there to guide us, and direct us into community, but we must first hold our faith in the Lord only. If you are avoiding going to church, or stopped going altogether over a negative experience, can I ask you to try again?

We must never give up because of a hurt experience.

God says, *"If you suffer as a Christian, do not be ashamed but praise God that you bear that name"* (1 Peter 4:16). The fact of the matter is, the church is not a building or a religion, it is us! Yes, we are the body of the church! "We are therefore Christ's ambassadors, as though God were making his appeal through us. We implore you on Christ's behalf: Be reconciled to God" (2 Corinthians 5:20). In 1 Corinthians 6:15, God asks, *"Do you know that your bodies are members of Christ himself?"*

We all have a part in the church as members. Romans 12:4–5 reminds us, *"Just as each of us has one body with many members, and these members do not all have the same function, so in Christ we who are many form one body, and each member belongs to all the others."* The church needs you. God wants you.

Dear Lord, I'm sorry that how, as a church, we can hurt each other. Help us to remember that You are our only hope, and we must do our part as the body of Christ. I pray that everyone reading this will get the resources they need to start a new relationship with You. I know You have been waiting for them with open arms. Thank You for the grace that You have given us all.

QUESTIONS FOR REFLECTION AND PERSONAL WORK

1.) Where have I been offended by the church?

_____

_____

_____

_____

_____

_____

2.) Am I willing to let this go and try again? Why or why not?

_____

_____

_____

_____

_____

_____

3.) Has my upbringing had a negative or positive influence on my journey with the Lord?

_____

_____

_____

_____

_____

_____

_____

4.) Do I believe it is important to go to church as a family?

_____

_____

_____

_____

_____

_____

5.) Am I willing to try to go to church as a family?

_____

_____

_____

_____

_____

_____

6.) If my family does not go to church, how could this influence my teen?

_____

_____

_____

_____

_____

_____

7.) I am committing to finding a new church near me.

_____

_____

_____

_____

_____

_____

Sign here: _____

CHAPTER 15:

SURRENDER

I am grateful that I built my relationship with the Lord before my cancer. I can remember I had a pretty good attitude and was not too terribly afraid, having faith that I would be fine in the end. I can remember that when the nurse wheeled me into surgery, I noticed that she was quiet and looked sad. I started to wonder if she felt bad about her patients, and I sensed some worry in her face, so I thought I would try some small talk. *"So do you ever watch E.R.?"* I asked her. *"Sometimes, but we tend to make fun of a lot of the diagnoses or treatments they talk about,"* she answered. We both chuckled a bit.

Surrender takes practice. Surrender is not giving up but laying our problems or desires at the Lord's feet and still being faithful in our prayers. Surrender is something that needs to be done daily, sometimes many times a day. It will be hard to surrender and trust God if you don't know Him on a personal level. You will not know God on a personal level unless you read His Word (the Bible). The more we realize God's love, the easier it is to surrender.

Surrendering will bring us a great amount of freedom, but it is not easy. Our pride and fear can constantly get in the way. We cannot fulfill God's purposes if we are only focused on our own plans. You will be tested on this. Do not give up, but surrender! It's the only way to recovery and peace. Talk about surrender with your kids. If they feel like giving up with something, ask them to pray and to surrender it to God.

Dear Lord, we completely surrender our fear and pain to You. We understand our way has not been working, and we are ready to see how You will "[work] for the good of those who love [you]" (Romans 8:28). We know we try to take control of situations and fail miserably. Thank you for Your promises. "Let us not become weary in doing good, for at the proper time we will reap a harvest if we do not give up" (Galatians 6:9).

QUESTIONS FOR REFLECTION AND PERSONAL WORK

1.) Where do I try to take control instead of surrendering to God and having more faith?

_____

_____

_____

_____

_____

_____

_____

2.) How can I show or model surrender behavior to my child?

_____

_____

_____

_____

_____

_____

_____

3.) Do I really believe God will care for me if I surrender my problems to Him?

_____

_____

_____

_____

_____

4.) Where have I surrendered in the past?

_____

_____

_____

_____

_____

_____

5.) What is preventing me from surrendering right now?

_____

_____

_____

_____

_____

CHAPTER 16:

LETTING OUR KIDS FEEL PAIN

Helping our kids build character is the hardest thing for us to do, but also the most important. If we protect our children from all difficult situations, God cannot grow them into the person He wants them to be. This always was and is a huge struggle for me. I want to protect my loved ones from all pain and hurt. It hurts our hearts to see our kids upset, especially in deep pain. Sometimes we need to be tough on our kids even if it pains us.

There is so much talk of how times are different with kids these days. Parents of kids in the seventies and eighties would kick them out the door to play until dinner time. Our kids these days spend hours and hours playing video games or scrolling through their phones. We really can do better, despite what is socially acceptable these days with electronics. I'm not saying video games are bad, but if we are letting those things babysit our kids, there will be negative consequences down the road.

Really though, if we want our kids to grow up to be respectful human beings, then it's up to us to do the hard work now. If you are going through a challenging season with your family, may I suggest reaching out to a friend or relative to put in a few hours with your child? Allowing our kids to have endless hours on their phones or social media before the age of eighteen is dangerous. Social media can have a negative effect on self-esteem, learning skills, depression, sleep disturbances, social skills, education, and overall mental health. Perhaps there can be a spot in the kitchen for plug-in times with phones, such as after school and during bedtime hours. Set rules and set boundaries.

It seems the more we give our child, the more it can backfire. The more "things" they have, the less they appreciate them. The more spoiled they are, the less likely they will work hard for what they want. The only thing we can give our children in unlimited amounts, and that will have a positive impact on them, is our time. Even if you sit there in silence, it gives your children the opportunity to talk about a problem if there is one there. You could even just ask them to take a walk.

Make a list of things you can do or talk about with your child so you can be intentional. Some of these things seem obvious, but once they become teenagers, they can feel so distant and we will need to put these practices into place more than ever.

Lastly, when we model godly behavior, we are giving

our kids the best gift we can give them. You may think they will think it's stupid, and if you're out of practice, it may feel stupid, but never underestimate how God will use you to influence your child. You can play Christian music at home, you can pray with them, you can ask them to pray for you! If they were not raised in a Christian home, it's never too late to start!

Dear Lord, You know better than anyone that I can be a real slacker when it comes to disciplining my kids. I'm sorry about this. Thank You for convicting me and helping me to allow my husband to help in this matter. Please help us to be strong and help us all to invest the time needed to raise mentally, socially, healthy kids.

Sometimes there are situations that are out of our hands, and we have done everything we could, and it still isn't enough. That's when I pray that we give it all over to You. We put our trust and faith in You. We know that you will not fail us. Raising children is a very high calling, and I pray we won't forget that. "Do not withhold discipline from a child; if you punish them with the rod, they will not die" (Proverbs 23:13).

QUESTIONS FOR REFLECTION AND PERSONAL WORK

1.) How do I react when my child is in pain?

_____

_____

_____

_____

_____

_____

2.) How do I react when my child needs to be disciplined?

_____

_____

_____

_____

_____

_____

3.) Was I raised strictly or not? How has this affected my parenting skills?

_____

_____

_____

_____

_____

_____

_____

4.) Will my child will be happier if I provide more things for them? Why or why not?

_____

_____

_____

_____

_____

5.) Would I have a better connection with my child if I spent more time with them?

_____

_____

_____

_____

_____

_____

6.) Am I on the same page with my spouse regarding how to discipline our child?

_____

_____

_____

_____

_____

_____

7.) Do we pray as a family?

_____

_____

_____

_____

_____

8.) How would my child's life improve with prayer?

_____

_____

_____

_____

_____

CHAPTER 17:

HUMILITY ABOVE ALL

We all want people to acknowledge and notice us, but isn't it so attractive when we meet a humble person? There is something so intriguing and beautiful about someone who is humble. When I see people go after dreams that are of fame or fortune, or just personal satisfaction, so often I see they are let down. It is important to have dreams and visions, but if they are not of God, then we must let them go. How do we know if they are from God, you may ask? For one, you could ask yourself if your dream or vision will help someone else.

God has a great deal to say about pride. When we can humble ourselves and make ourselves vulnerable, many people can relate to us and learn from us. God wants us to tell each other our stories, no matter how ugly. When we tell God our shortcomings, we are forgiven, but when we tell each other, we are healed!

When we can learn from our lessons, God will meet us in the middle of our pain, and not only perfect us, but increase our compassion for the suffering of others. When we don't apply our lessons, God will continue to strip us of our pride repeatedly, one painful experience after the next. It all boils down to pride!

Dear Lord, help us to get the confidence You want us to have and the humility at the same time. You deserve to see a glorious bright light shining from within so that when people ask where that light is coming from, we can proclaim Your greatness! "For the LORD will be at your side and will keep your foot from being snared" (Proverbs 3:26). "Pride goes before destruction, a haughty spirit before a fall" (Proverbs 16:18).

Help us to have that balancing act of confidence with humility. Forgive us for being selfish and concentrating on ourselves. May we be like little children, humbling ourselves so that we may be great in Your kingdom (Matthew 18: 3–4). Help us to model humble behavior for our children.

QUESTIONS FOR REFLECTION AND PERSONAL WORK

1.) Where has my pride gotten in the way of peace?

_____

_____

_____

_____

_____

_____

_____

2.) Where can I admit that I have been wrong to my child?

_____

_____

_____

_____

_____

_____

_____

3.) Do I notice pride in other people and not in myself?

_____

_____

_____

_____

_____

_____

4.) Do I have a hard time saying I'm sorry?

_____

_____

_____

_____

_____

_____

5.) Will I try to admit when I am wrong?

_____

_____

_____

_____

_____

_____

CHAPTER 18:

THE ENEMY IS ON THE PROWL

Why is it that we can cry out to God in desperation and pain, (as we all should) but never scream out to the impostor, the evil spirit, the devil, the tempter? He is your enemy, by whatever name you feel comfortable using. I always knew there was such a person; but it seemed too scary to talk about and maybe I would be giving credit where credit wasn't due if I acknowledged his existence. The fact is, we have an evil force in this world just as we have a good force (God) and until we face him head-on instead of ignoring him, then he will continue to poke at our weaknesses.

We all have our weaknesses. Unfortunately, the evil one knows just how to get to those weaknesses and play on them. The evil one knows the struggle of alcoholism with my family and has tempted them for years. The evil one knows how much I hate winters and have dealt with seasonal depression for years. So, what are we to do?

First, we must build our relationship with God. When Christ is in our hearts, the imposter has only as much power as we allow. *"Put on the full armor of God so that you can take your stand against the devil's schemes"* (Ephesians 6:11). It is a matter of getting stern, as if you were a parent disciplining a child. If you are like me and not very stern when it comes to parenting, you must change. This is no place for wimpy discipline. It's not easy when we have a stronghold, such as addictions, *but "God is faithful; he will not let you be tempted beyond what you can bear. But when you are tempted, he will also provide a way out so that you can endure it"* (1 Corinthians 10:13).

"Your enemy the devil prowls around like a roaring lion looking for someone to devour. Resist him, standing firm in the faith, because you know that the family of believers throughout the world is undergoing the same kind of sufferings" (1 Peter 5:8–9). So, stand up, telling him firmly, there is no place for him; no room in the inn! He must leave at once because you are a person of God and God always wins!

Dear Lord, I know You have given authority "over the enemy" (Luke 10:19), so I command the evil one to leave at once. We refuse to listen to him! Thank You for having power over what we acknowledge and pray for. Please release any strongholds over anyone who is reading this. Thank You that we can overcome even generational sin with Your love and Spirit. Freedom is right around the corner; I can see it! Thank You for reminding us that, "Blessed is the one who perseveres under trial because, having stood the test, that person will receive the crown of life that the Lord has promised to those who love him" (James 1:12).

QUESTIONS FOR REFLECTION AND PERSONAL WORK

1.) Do I think there is such a thing as an evil spirit? Why or why not?

_____

_____

_____

_____

_____

_____

2.) What are my biggest temptations or strongholds I need to overcome?

_____

_____

_____

_____

_____

_____

3.) Who can I talk to about these? If I have no one, will I commit to finding someone?

_____

_____

_____

_____

_____

_____

4.)What do I see my child being tempted with that is not of God?

_____

_____

_____

_____

_____

5.) Will I talk to my child about things that tempt me?

_____

_____

_____

_____

_____

_____

6.) Will I commit to finding a mentor (outside of the family) for my child?

_____

_____

_____

_____

_____

_____

CHAPTER 19:

THERE IS HOPE

The unimaginable happened to our family. One of our sons was bullied in school by teachers—yes, teachers! As he grew, this had more of an effect on him than we could have known. Then we hit the perfect storm. Because of the difficulty of the teen years, along with my seasonal depression and my husband losing his job, we were unable to be there for our son emotionally and it all blew up in our face. We felt our sweet son slipping away from us.

At first, we thought it was just a rebellion and then it turned dangerous. It was such a scary time for us. I felt God pressing on my heart to enroll our son at Teen Challenge, a center designed to help teens with emotional and recovery needs. One of the most devastating things a family could go through ended up being one of the most amazing experiences and blessings. One thing the staff there said repeatedly is that they see the most amazing parents come through their doors. So, stop feeling guilty. Just because you are going through a rough time with your child does not mean you are a bad parent!

We had our heads down at the altar that year and God did much-needed work in our family. At the end of Teen Challenge, our son went on to enroll at Youth With A Mission training (YWAM). We are so proud to see how this boy turned into a thriving young man. He went on to get married, got a great job as a sous-chef, and bought his first house at age twenty-one!

I can say now that I am grateful for such an experience because we were able to live the life Christ wants for us. If I didn't know the Lord and didn't hear the promptings, our son might be dead. If you are going through a difficult season, take drastic measures. Pray and seek godly counsel. There is hope with the Lord. Let Him do his work, and He will do immeasurably more than you could ever ask or imagine according to His power that is at work within us. To Him be the glory and in the church and in Christ Jesus! (See Ephesians 3:20–21.)

Dear Lord, I pray right now for the families that are struggling for unity and peace. I pray that they will give their hearts to You if they do not know You. I pray that You will do the work in them that they need. Thank You that there is hope in You even in the most painful experiences. I pray that when these families can overcome these trying times, they will tell their stories. "And if the spirit of him who raised Jesus from the dead is living in you, he who raised Christ from the dead will also give life to your mortal bodies because of his spirit who lives in you" (Romans 8:11).

QUESTIONS AND REFLECTION FOR PERSONAL WORK

1.) Where have I felt like I have lost hope?

_____

_____

_____

_____

_____

_____

2.) Have I accepted Jesus Christ as my Lord and Savior?

_____

_____

_____

_____

_____

_____

3.) If my ways have not been working for me, am I willing to give God's way a try?

_____

_____

_____

5.)   Do I believe there is hope with God's love and power?

6.) Am I willing to die to self to have a new beginning with God?

Reflect on what that means.

CHAPTER 20:

TRUST IS A MUST

Everything we do to become a better version of ourselves does not give us a free pass into Heaven. God saved us by His grace when we believed. This is a gift from God, and no one can take credit for this. "Salvation is not a reward for the good things we have done, so none of us can boast about it, for we are God's masterpiece. He created us a new in Christ Jesus, so we can do the good things He planned for us long ago" (Ephesians 2:9–10, NLT).

There are no works that we can do to earn God's favor, no matter how many good things we try to do or how good of a person we try to be. The thing God wants the most from us is our trust! When we believe and trust, God will move in our lives. This is good news that God already loves us no matter what we have done. Trying to do good deeds is about living in peace, knowing you are glorifying God, living His way and not your own. The intent behind our actions should be love, and that is what God is at the core. Our trust is expressed when we can live in peace, even when things are at their worst, knowing that God is working! Now on the other side of trust, taking electronics from our teens at night does not mean we don't trust them. It just means we don't trust what is coming after them. I would strongly advise this practice. You will get a lot of heat from your teen about this, but until they are eighteen, you have the right to put protective practices in place.

Dear Lord, thank You for loving our broken selves. Thank You for never giving up on us when our trust fades. Thank You that when we trust and have faith in You, you are able to do things that are far beyond anything we could ever imagine, for "just as the heavens are higher than the earth, so are Your ways higher than our ways, and Your thoughts higher than our thoughts (Isaiah 55:8–9). I pray that You will help us keep our eyes focused on You and our faith strong. I pray that You will help others hear Your voice, and that Your purposes be fulfilled. You are the way and the truth and the life. No one comes to the Father except through You (John 14:6).

QUESTIONS FOR REFLECTION AND PERSONAL WORK

1.) Do I trust God to take care of my needs? Why or why not?

_____

_____

_____

_____

_____

_____

_____

2.) Do I have anyone in my life I fully trust?

_____

_____

_____

_____

_____

_____

_____

3.) Is there anyone in my child's life they can trust?

_____

_____

_____

4.) Does my child trust me? If not, how can you change that?

5.) I will commit to putting trustworthy individuals in my child's life.

CHAPTER 21:

WORRY IS WORTHLESS

Worry and anxiety can get the best of us, robbing us of peace and of being able to live for God. Anxiety is at an all-time high for our teens. Worry is definitely the work of Satan. He can keep our minds so filled with it that it can paralyze us from living God's will for our lives. Worrying about someone is not a prayer or a compliment. It is only saying you do not trust God to answer your prayers.

Teenager's brains are changing as well as their bodies. They want more independence and autonomy, but they may not be ready for it. Because of social media, teenagers have more to worry about than we, their parents, ever had. Anxiety can be a normal emotion such as being angry or embarrassed, but when anxiety stops them from doing everyday things, it needs to be addressed.

What can we do besides prayer to help with our worry or anxiety? For one, we can acknowledge it. Ignoring or dismissing strong emotions by saying, *"Everything will be okay,"* or *"You have a good life,"* will not help. Remind them that many other kids feel the same way and are dealing with the same emotions. Of course, having the door open to always listen (not talk) is helpful.

Encourage healthy activities to keep their minds clear, such as sports and hobbies. Small groups for teens are very healthy because it can be a safe circle to hear of anxieties that others may already be dealing with, and be able to hear others express how they are feeling. It helps them to not feel weird or abnormal. Building your family circle of trusted friends and mentors is crucial.

Dear Lord, I'm sorry for all the worthless worry we have done in the past. Please help those teens that have anxiety to feel Your presence and feel Your love. It breaks my heart to know of all the social media our kids need to deal with that may be zapping their self-confidence and I know it breaks Your heart too.

Protect those who love You, Father. Please release worry from those who are reading this. Continue to help us with resources that we need. Thank You for Your Word. "Therefore do not worry about tomorrow, for tomorrow will worry about itself. Each day has enough trouble of its own" (Matthew 6:34).

QUESTIONS FOR REFLECTION AND PERSONAL WORK

1.) What am I most worried about? Can I give this over to God now?

_____

_____

_____

_____

_____

_____

_____

2.) What does my child seem to worry or have anxiety about?

_____

_____

_____

_____

_____

_____

_____

3.) Has worrying ever helped me?

_____

_____

_____

_____

_____

_____

_____

4.) Can I stretch my faith on this subject?

_____

_____

_____

_____

_____

_____

5.) Is there a group I can help my child get involved in to hear other's struggles?

_____

_____

_____

_____

_____

_____

CHAPTER 22:

HOLD OUR TONGUES

Probably one of the hardest skills to learn is to hold our tongue. I especially see people these days spewing out political opinions as if everyone else agrees with them. After all, especially in politics, it is just an opinion, not a right or wrong. It takes a disciplined and humble person to always remember this. Our opinions are not better than someone else's—they are just different.

We are not always going to agree with our children's opinions, especially as they age and turn into teens. Some things they say may even sound downright dumb, but this is where we can practice holding our tongue. They need to be heard. Listen! Let them speak their peace and then explain in love why they may be wrong. I'm sorry folks but, *"because I said so"* is not good enough! We can do better! Give them eye contact and don't think about what you are going to say next while they are talking!

Being kind is so underrated! When we practice being kind with our words, we put ourselves in a position to be ready to be loved and to give love. Let's face it, sometimes teens are hard to love when they speak of ridiculous things, but remember, they may have heard something from a friend or on social media. Instead of ridiculing them, ask them why they feel that way. They may realize they don't even know why.

I'm sorry, but the stupidest saying I have ever heard is... *"sticks and stones may break my bones, but words will never hurt me."* B-A-L-O-G-N-A! How wrong is that! James 1:26 tells us that *"those who consider themselves religious and yet do not keep a tight rein on their tongues deceive themselves, and their religion is worthless."*

We all have our pressure points. With some, its politics, others religion, or some relational or family issues. Whatever your pressure points are, note them, so you can be better prepared to hold your tongue when the topic arises. *"Sin is not ended by multiplying words, but the prudent hold their tongues"* (Proverbs 10:19).

Dear Lord, we are so quick to speak sometimes. Forgive us for the words that have been said that hurt people, especially our children. We know we can do better, and we will try.... every day. Right now, Lord, we also forgive those who have hurt us with their words. Thank You that You are such a good God and want the best for us, even when we don't act our best. Amen.

QUESTIONS FOR REFLECTION AND PERSONAL WORK

1.) Would my child say I am a good listener?

_____

_____

_____

_____

_____

_____

_____

2.) When is it the hardest to hold my tongue?

_____

_____

_____

_____

_____

_____

_____

3.) When do I think people really need to hear my opinion?

_____

_____

_____

4.) How can I model good listening skills for my child?

5.) Which is the hardest subject or pressure point to hold my tongue?

6.) Do I think my relationship with my child would improve if I were more careful with my words?

_____

_____

_____

_____

_____

_____

_____

CHAPTER 23:

DO YOUR WEEDING

There are always going to be negative people who, unfortunately, will come into our lives. People who always see their glass as half-empty can be exhausting to be around, but they may be just lacking in faith. The kind of people that I am talking about, and you should pull out of your lives like weeds, are toxic people. They are people that intimidate you or bully you in such a way that you are oppressed. I had a toxic work environment at a hospital, and I eventually had to quit. I loved the job, but it was breaking my soul to see how people were treated. If you have a coworker, teacher, friend, or anyone else in your life that is depleting your joy and hope, then I suggest you pull the weeds! I know it's not always easy with family or coworkers, but the damage may not be worth your investment.

Let's face it, every family has its share of dysfunction. If you don't think so, then you are fooling yourself. A little bit of crazy is normal. What you really need to analyze is if the relationship can be restored, and can that person change? If so, there is hope. My family had its share of dysfunction, but my parents were great encouragers. They always told me I could do whatever I wanted, and they said it enough until I believed them!

In my adult life I have definitely run across more negativity, but you know if I listened to every person who didn't share my vision or dreams, I would still probably be depressed. People don't have to share your vision or dream, but you need to draw the line when they are giving out negative counsel. Children often have dreams that are very out of touch with reality, and that's okay! The worst thing you could do is squash that. Encourage those dreams no matter how farfetched they seem! After all, a dream is just a dream for kids and sometimes they can surprise everyone!

Dear Lord, please help us to seek smart, godly counsel. Help us to be brave and weed the negativity out of our lives. Help your children to take control and not let one more thing burden their hearts. Help us to distance themselves from those who drain us. Help us to rely more on You and Your Word. You are the wonderful counselor! "Blessed is the one who does not walk in step with the wicked or stand in the way that sinners take or sit in the company of mockers" (Psalm 1:1).

QUESTIONS FOR REFLECTION AND PERSONAL WORK

1.) Who do I know that I need to weed out of my life?

_____

_____

_____

_____

_____

_____

2.) What is it going to take to do that?

_____

_____

_____

_____

_____

3.) Who does my child need to weed out of their life? Ask them.

_____

_____

_____

_____

_____

_____

_____

4.) Will this take drastic measures, such as moving? Am I willing to do such things to bring peace to my family?

_____

_____

_____

_____

_____

_____

5.) Who can I seek for godly counsel? If I don't know, I will commit to searching for that today.

_____

_____

_____

_____

_____

_____

CHAPTER 24:

WHAT BRINGS YOU TO YOUR KNEES?

Do you have anything that brings you to your knees? For instance, do you feel your heart stop when you see or hear about neglected animals, or feel your legs go weak when you see or hear of starving children? There should be something that you feel extremely passionate about. This is what I mean about bringing you to your knees. If you do not feel strongly about anything, please don't live that way. A good place to start if you honestly don't feel strongly about something is to reflect on where your greatest pain has been.

To live out our purpose, we need to have a vision. To have a vision, we need to know what our passion is. To know what our passion is, we need to know what brings us to our knees. This may need some deep reflection. Perhaps you grew up in an abusive home, and instead of burying it, you can use this to fuel your passion. Maybe you are a cancer survivor—put that pain to purpose! When we show passion to our children, it allows them to feel okay with being passionate.

We are passionate beings that are meant to feel deeply so we can love deeply. It is not an advantage to always be cool as a cucumber. Love, compassion, and passion can drive us to do beautiful things. This is the root of Christianity—to love passionately! Does your child show passion towards something? There are ways you can help with that. Getting on your knees and crying yourself clean is not a sign of weakness; it's a sign you are passionate or feel deeply about something.

Dear Lord, thank You for creating us to be passionate and compassionate beings. Help us to channel our passion into helping the injustice in this world. I pray everyone reading this will find a passion that will bring them to their knees. You are the ultimate example of compassion. You felt so bad for what we were turning into that you sent your only Son to save us.

> *Therefore if you have any encouragement from being united with Christ, if any comfort from his love, if any common sharing in the Spirit, if any tenderness and compassion, then make my joy complete by being like-minded, having the same love, being one in spirit and of one mind.*
>
> **Philippians 2:1–2**

QUESTIONS FOR REFLECTION AND PERSONAL WORK

1.) Do I have something that brings me to my knees? If not, I will take some time for reflection on my pain in the past.

_____

_____

_____

_____

_____

_____

2.) Do I feel like being passionate about something, and having something *"bring you to your knees,"* is the same thing? Why or why not?

_____

_____

_____

_____

_____

_____

_____

PEACE AND PURPOSE FOR PARENTS WITH TEENS

3.) Does my child have anything they are passionate about?

_____

_____

_____

_____

_____

_____

4.) How can I help my child to feel compassion for the injustice?

_____

_____

_____

_____

_____

_____

5.) Do I think it's healthy to have my child see me cry? Why or why not?

_____

_____

_____

_____

WHAT BRINGS YOU TO YOUR KNEES?

_____

_____

_____

CHAPTER 25:

ELECTRONICS

I know I have touched on electronics, but if we as parents can get this one topic right, it can save everyone a great deal of heartache. If you have bought the phone, and pay for the phone bill monthly, why do you feel you can't be in control of your teen's phone? If your child is under the age of eighteen, you should have total control of their phone.

What I mean by this is, if they don't answer your calls or texts, you should be able to shut down all their use of controls by an app. You should be able to download a tracking or GPS app that will allow you to know where they are at any given time. You can put an app on the phone that allows you to see ALL texts coming through. If you think this sounds harsh, then you may not understand or know the reality of the kind of damage that can be done through their devices.

I was just at a youth parent night at our church and a mother described how her daughter would physically throw up if her phone was taken away. This does not surprise me one bit.

We had no idea how bad our situation was until we placed an app on our son's phone and read some of the texts that were coming through. Unfortunately, our kids have found their identity in their phones, and to physically get sick over having their phones taken away shows what is mastering them. Somehow or other we must help them realize that.

One way we can help is not by having our own devices master us. I understand there is a need for business, but when your teens are around, put down your phone, turn off the TV, and be available to listen.

Talk with your teen about what it means to communicate with others using expressions and body language. This may sound bad, but we may have to teach our teens how to talk to others. It may not come naturally to them if they have had phones since an early age. They are used to using their fingers, not their mouths, to talk to others.

I have noticed teens feeling awkward around each other when their answers must come out of their mouths. I recently saw a group of teens at a Starbucks sitting next to one another and texting. No one was saying anything to each other, and I wouldn't be surprised if they were texting each other. This is very foreign and strange to my generation, but unfortunately, it is becoming widely acceptable.

If there is one thing I hope you get out of this book, it is that you feel not only empowered, but do what is necessary to take control of your teen's phone. Please do your research on the latest apps and then share it with other parents! *"Always give yourselves fully to the work of the Lord, because you know that your labor in the Lord is not in vain"* (1 Corinthians 15:58).

CHAPTER 26:

DISCIPLINE

There are so many areas that need our attention and discipline. We need to discipline our eyes, our ears, our mouth, and our hands! We can't do this without help from God. All of us are weak, at least in one area of our life. The good news is, we don't have to be defeated. We can kick that habit, or lose that weight, or start that business with our power of faith. Discipline is so important, but not easy!

For teens, we often think the more disciplined, the more they will rebel, but this is just the opposite. Clearly defined boundaries will help them feel safe. This is so incredibly important. So are responsibilities. If we don't prepare our teens for responsibility now, we will have to watch them suffer as adults. Even being disciplined with our time is important, as we only have so much time each day.

May I suggest coming up with a contract for both you and your child? Talk out what you both feel is fair for curfews, phone use, friend groups, communication, and anything else you feel would be helpful to be united as a family. Every home is different, and every person is different. If you are just hoping and praying your child will just do everything that you ask, then you may be fooling yourself. Take baby steps and give lots of praise to your child for even small wins. How about yourself? Are there habits and hang-ups that you need to address so you can be emotionally available to your child? What is not talked about cannot be expected, so this is the time to really be open with yourself and your child.

If there is one area that we need to get better at disciplining our children in, it is the use of phones and computers. If you think you have more of an influence over your child than their phones and computers, then you may need a wake-up call. Technology is a blessing and a curse at the same time. There must be discipline in this area, no exceptions. If I could raise my boys all over again, this is the number one area of concern I would have. *"The fear of the Lord is the beginning of knowledge, but fools despise wisdom and discipline"* (Proverbs 1:7).

Dear Lord, we fail so many times at trying to be disciplined that we sometimes wonder if it's worth it. But it is worth all the effort we give towards disciplining our mind, body, and soul! Thank You for saying that it really is possible with faith. We are becoming a new person. Please help those who are struggling with discipline. In Jesus' name, amen

QUESTIONS FOR REFLECTION AND PERSONAL WORK

1.) What are some habits, hang ups, and addictions I need to be more disciplined with?

_____

_____

_____

_____

_____

_____

_____

2.) What is an area of discipline I cannot seem to apply to my child?

_____

_____

_____

_____

_____

_____

3.) Are there new boundaries that need to be established? What are they?

_____

_____

_____

_____

_____

_____

4.) How would my family life change if we were both more disciplined?

_____

_____

_____

_____

_____

5.) If my spouse is better at disciplining our child, am I willing to let them take the lead?

_____

_____

_____

_____

_____

_____

6.) Does my child have limited and supervised use of their phones and computers? If not, I can start now.

_____

_____

_____

_____

_____

_____

_____

CHAPTER 27

PATIENCE IS A TEST

Have you ever prayed to God to give you more patience, and then He just gives you more to be patient about? We must remember God can make any circumstance better in due time. Sometimes what we pray for is not always in our best interest, even though we think it is. God may see a better path that we cannot.

Praying for God's will and then having faith He will work it out will help us with our unrest. God is doing some work in your life right now, and perhaps in your child's life. He is building your character and helping you become more like Christ. He is paving the way for something much bigger than you could ever know. With faith, trust, and humility, you will get there and see the purpose of your pain someday. God is trying to see just how much you trust Him.

God is not glorified with your suffering, but He is glorified with your patience and trust during your suffering. *"Let perseverance finish its work so that you may be mature and complete, not lacking anything"* (James 1: 4). Patience is definitely a skill that takes time to learn. With that being said, give some grace to your kids who lack patience.

Dear Lord, thank You for Your promises on having patience. We pray that we will have good attitudes as we wait on Your promises. It is so amazing today how You answer such big prayers in big ways. It is very clear You are still at work in Your universe today. I pray that those reading this today will not lose heart and grow weary and faint in being noble and doing right, for in due time and appointed season we shall reap, if we do not lose our courage and grow faint (Galatians 6:9).

QUESTIONS FOR REFLECTION AND PERSONAL WORK

1.) What am I having to be patient about today?

_____

_____

_____

_____

_____

_____

2.) Do I feel I have developed good patience skills?

_____

_____

_____

_____

_____

_____

3.) What is my child being patient about? How can I pray for him/her?

_____

_____

_____

_____

_____

_____

_____

4.) Do I feel if I am patient, God will work all things out for my good?

_____

_____

_____

_____

_____

5.) Where can I model better patience skills for my child?

_____

_____

_____

_____

_____

_____

CHAPTER 28:

DREAMS AND VISIONS

A major contributor to being stuck at the same place in our lives is being stuck in a dream. We don't feel worthy enough just being ourselves, so we dream of great things and feel that when we finally reach our dream, then we'll be happy. The problem is, sometimes we never start that dream because of fear or just the fact that it is so much fun dreaming about it. If we go after our dream and we don't succeed, then we feel our life is not worthy. I've had so many ideas through the years of sharing my passions, but my standards were too high, and I feared failure. I wanted everything to go so perfectly that I never really started for years. Sound familiar?

There I was, like so many, stuck in my own dream. At one point this intensified my depression. Somewhere God gave me the vision, and I started to believe that my life could be what I dreamed. We are such a society of, *"I want it, and I want it now."* If you don't love the process of your dream, then you may have the wrong dream. It takes a lot of hard work and grit, and when you start to love the process, the dream will follow! I believe this to be true of money as well. If your only motive is to make money, you may very well make lots of money, but you will be unfulfilled. Putting your life to purpose will bring you fulfillment and then the money will naturally come if that is best for you.

It is important to have visions and dreams, of course, but once we appreciate our current circumstances, we can start doing something about it! Has God birthed a new vision for you? Awesome! Pursuing a vision will require great faith. A vision should always be a solution to a problem. God is using your circumstances and experiences to prepare you for His vision for your life. I am convinced that people who are stuck in their life will never truly get unstuck without some vision.

Because God created all nature, sometimes we can get better visions when spending time in His creation, the outdoors. For some people, it is water and the beach or the mountains and trees. Think about how you like to spend time in the outdoors and go there! Have a heart-to-heart talk with God and tell Him you are searching for a vision for your life. If your dream and vision is to just have a healthy family, then focus on that. I have been there, time and time again.

Dear Lord, thank You for preparing our way! "You were taught, with regard to your former way of life, to put off your old self, which is being corrupted by its deceitful desires; to be made new in the attitude of your minds; and to put on the new self, created to be like God in true righteousness and holiness" (Ephesians 4:22–24) Thank You for families reading this who want to make You proud. You know their hearts, Lord. Thank You for the beautiful world You created for our pleasure. There is so much You have done for us to have pleasure and I am in awe of You. Amen.

QUESTIONS FOR REFLECTION AND PERSONAL WORK

1.) What is something I have always dreamed of doing? Would that make God proud?

_____

_____

_____

_____

_____

_____

_____

2.) What am I good at but feel it is too big of a task to turn into a purpose?

_____

_____

_____

_____

_____

_____

3.) Am I able to influence many people? Morale influence is essential!

_____

_____

_____

_____

_____

_____

_____

4.) How can I share a dream with my child? How can I share a dream with my parents?

_____

_____

_____

_____

_____

5.) How have I suffered? Can I start to share my story?

_____

_____

_____

_____

_____

_____

CHAPTER 29:

LIVING WITH BROKEN RELATIONSHIPS

Parents that have to live in a divorce situation will have extra challenges, but that doesn't mean you can no longer live or parent well! This will take incredible discipline on your part. Your partner may have really wronged you and deserve all your wrath, but is that fair to your kids? Kids who turn into adults often talk about the trauma they had living with divorced parents. Wouldn't that be amazing to have your kids witness pleasant exchanges for their sake? Wouldn't that be an amazing gift of peace for your child? You may be thinking, but I do try. My ex doesn't. Well, that's all you can do is worry about yourself and your child. You cannot control your ex or their actions, but you can control your own. God will notice your efforts, even if your ex doesn't.

When you speak of your ex in a degrading way in front of your child, that does not give them insight as to how you feel, it only gives them anxiety. Just as God understands your challenges you have faced; God also understands your motives. I can only imagine how hard this must be, but instead of talking about your ex in front of your child, try talking about it in a support group. So many people are in your situation. You are not alone.

Even couples with the strongest marriages will not always agree on how to raise their children, so somehow there needs to be that added compromise and work to help raise healthy individuals. Even if you can't stand the sight or voice of your ex, commit to peaceful exchanges for your child and, ultimately, for God. I'm so sorry that you have this to deal with, but I can promise you, with God's help, there is hope for restoration.

Dear Lord, divorce is so hard on families. I know You have already forgiven them, so there is no need for guilt! Just the desire and need to want to do better for their children. Thank You that You can restore even the most broken relationships. I pray all parents can try for Your sake to make peace with their ex and that their children will benefit from such hard work. "I appeal to you, brothers, in the name of our Lord Jesus Christ, that all of you agree with one another so that there may be no divisions among you" (1 Corinthians 1:10).

QUESTIONS FOR REFLECTION AND PERSONAL WORK

1.) Do I feel I have been doing all I can to keep peace with my ex?

_____

_____

_____

_____

_____

_____

_____

2.) Would God be proud of the way I treat my ex?

_____

_____

_____

_____

_____

_____

_____

3.) Does my relationship with my ex brings anxiety to my child?

_____

_____

_____

_____

_____

_____

_____

4.) If my relationship with my ex is under strain, will I commit to seeking professional help, even if it's just for me and my child?

_____

_____

_____

_____

_____

5.) How can I show love to someone I dislike for my child's well-being?

_____

_____

_____

_____

_____

_____

CHAPTER 30:

HOW DO I FIND PURPOSE?

There have been entire books written on purpose, and rightfully so! It is so important for everyone to feel purpose. If we don't have a purpose, all it will take is a cloudy day or a nasty word from someone to put us into a tailspin. When we have a purpose, we wake up with joy and go to sleep feeling fulfilled. Everyone's journey to finding their purpose will look different. Some know from a very early age what they want to do, such as become a doctor, but that is a job, not a purpose. A job can certainly turn into a purpose, but there is a difference. A job will always have money exchanged, purpose may or may not.

Purpose is when your job, duty, or hobby aligns with your gifts and what your Creator designed for you. Jobs may or may not be fulfilling, but a purpose always will be. If you don't know what your gifts are, there are many ways to find that out. Gifts are generally something you are good at or enjoy doing, such as serving people, cooking, organizing, or fixing things. Many times, people are good at multiple things. When your gifts align with what your Creator designed for you, then you will have purpose.

Our Creator designed us so unique and so special. We may have similar gifts or jobs as others, but no one can quite do it the way you do. We often find purpose through our most painful experiences. When we understand how we have overcome those experiences with God's hand in play, we will see our purpose. When we live a purposeful life, it helps us model purpose for our children.

A specific example would be if someone overcame a difficult divorce and had a gift of teaching, perhaps they would teach or lead a divorce care group. Another example would be if someone lost their husband and they had a gift for cooking, perhaps they could cook meals for newly widowed individuals. To be honest, my purpose was staring me in the face for years and I ignored it due to fear. I wrote a book like this one fifteen years ago and never shared it. What a shame to miss out on purpose for so many years!

If we were put on this planet to worship and please God and reflect His glory, then living out our purpose will please Him and also please ourselves. It's hard to put such an important topic into a few short paragraphs, but I promise you the more you get to know God as your Friend and Savior, the clearer your purpose will be. Remember, the right purpose will always honor God, no matter what.

Dear Lord, it's never too early or too late for a person to find his purpose. I pray that you and your child can find purpose because purpose is what will give us "peace that surpasses all understanding" (Philippians 4:7). Bring the people into our lives, Lord, that can help reveal our purpose to us and our children. In Jesus' name, amen.

QUESTIONS FOR REFLECTION AND PERSONAL WORK

1.) What am I good at, or what do people say I'm good at?

_____

_____

_____

_____

_____

_____

2.) What do I enjoy doing? This could be a hobby or a job or even something as simple as taking walks.

_____

_____

_____

_____

_____

_____

4.) What kind of difficult things have I had to endure or overcome?

_____

_____

_____

_____

_____

_____

_____

5.) What is my biggest challenge to finding my purpose?

_____

_____

_____

_____

_____

_____

6.) Do I have an idea of what my purpose may be? If so, what are some next steps I can take?

_____

_____

_____

_____

_____

_____

7.) How can I encourage one another in my family to find their purpose?

_____

_____

_____

_____

_____

_____

_____

CHAPTER 31:

THE PUSHBACK

When you choose to live for God, you will always have those that do not agree with such a lifestyle or teachings. The pushback will come in many forms. One will be rationalization. You will hear such things (about unhealthy things) as, *"Everybody is doing it."* This will especially come from teens. You may also hear, *"We are living in a modern new age. Get with the times."* You will also hear justification, such as, *"You just don't understand the kind of pressure I'm in."* Or minimizing their behavior, such as, *"It's not so bad."* Another one that I get often is intellectualizing. They will try to say, *"In my research I have found ..."*

The most concerning and probably most dangerous pushback is silence or withdrawal. This is still a pushback, but it's similar to passive-aggressive behavior and can be very dangerous because it's hard to tell just how much someone is suffering. This is what we encountered with our son and did not know how bad it was until it was really bad! When a teen says, *"I don't want to talk about it,"* it may just mean they don't want to talk to you and that's okay! Find someone they will. Many therapists will assure teens of the confidentiality laws they have in place and will help them feel safe to share. We still do not know to this day what our son shared with professionals, and I'm good with that.

You will have to start navigating that pushback and how some people will not share or be open to your beliefs. This is not where you write them off, this is where you dig in, not with your words, but with your love. It's time we live by example, not out of fear or obligation, but out of worship pouring out of our hearts.

When you finally say yes to God and stop listening to the noise around you, everything will start falling into place. *"See to it that no one takes you captive through hollow and deceptive philosophy, which depends on human tradition and the elemental spiritual forces of this world rather than on Christ"* (Colossians 2:8).

Dear Lord, I pray for strength and courage for everyone that gets pushback. May they rely on Your Word and not on their own understanding. I pray for families of teens that have disbelief of You in their lives. I pray that You will penetrate their hearts in such a way that they will overflow with thanksgiving. I pray they will find the mentors and therapists and programs needed to bring them back to a healthy state. Thank You for how much You love them.

QUESTIONS FOR REFLECTION AND PERSONAL WORK

1.) Who will give pushback in my life?

_____

_____

_____

_____

_____

_____

_____

2.) Who will give pushback in my teen's life?

_____

_____

_____

_____

_____

_____

3.) Do I believe this statement: _"God loves you at whatever every stage of development you are in?"_

_____

_____

_____

_____

_____

_____

_____

4.) Do I believe in this statement: *"It's not how much pleasure I can get out of life, but how much pleasure I can bring to God?"*

_____

_____

_____

_____

_____

_____

5.) Am I willing to commit to finding a professional my teen can talk to?

_____

_____

_____

_____

_____

_____

CHAPTER 32:

PERSEVERANCE AND THE HOLY SPIRIT

When we are filled with the Holy Spirit, we can do the impossible. The Holy Spirit is our intercessor (Romans 8:26). The more we surrender, the more the Holy Spirit takes over (Ezekiel 36:27). We need the Spirit in our hearts because everything will go where our heart is: time, money, our words, and our efforts. The Holy Spirit wants to teach us who Christ is.

You will need to realize that what matters to people does not always impress God. People who follow others will get lost in that pursuit and will miss out on God's will for their lives. This is where we need to reach deep and rely on the Holy Spirit.

We were not all meant to be preachers, or writers, or Christian singers. Don't confuse what it means to have a purpose from God. Ask the Holy Spirit to guide you. God chose the uniqueness of your personality, not just your race and the color of your skin. God is in the design field, and He doesn't make any mistakes. God loved you so much that He wanted to take a bit from you and create another human being using that part. Just because your teen is not living well does not mean he was not perfectly made, because he was!

When your family and teen get to a healthy place, you will need aftercare. You will need great perseverance to not let things fall back to the way they were. Sadly, this often happens to families. Talking openly about how you have changed will be your testimony! You should never be ashamed of your testimony.

Many things in the future may need to see drastic changes. I know that when our son was done with Teen Challenge, we moved to another state, so he did not return to the same friends, teachers, and life that was unhealthy. These are the huge sacrifices you may need to make. Here are some areas for your family to put into a family contract:

1. Mentor—therapist schedule

2. Support group

3. Church attendance

4. School plans (home school?)

5. Computer, phone, and car usage

6. Personal growth plan

7. Family and friend time

8. Extracurricular activities

9. Employment

10. Ongoing drug testing

Dear Lord, I know it can be overwhelming for families, but with You and the Holy Spirit, nothing is impossible. Help them not only get the support they need, but to find their purpose. Help us to "forget the former things; do not dwell on the past. See I am doing a new thing" (Isaiah 43:18–19)! "The Lord will guide you always; he will satisfy your needs...you will be like a well-watered garden, like a spring whose waters never fail" (Isaiah 58:11).

CHAPTER 33:

WORSHIP

Worship is far more than music. Even sitting in silence can be an act of worship if we are seeking to hear from God. God loves most kinds of worship and most kinds of music. We can even listen to rock and roll and still sing praises to God. Worship is not for our benefit; we worship for God's benefit. It doesn't matter how you sing or what you sound like, God loves it all. God just wants the song that's in your heart.

These days teens are looking for any way they can escape reality, and can we hardly blame them? Music is huge for teens, and some have their ear buds in their ears all day long. Young people rely on music to make them feel good. Wouldn't you rather them be singing about a better way, rather than them singing about who's grinding who? I mean really, some secular music can be so raunchy. Worship music can take the attention off of themselves and recognize those around them. When this happens, then they are moving toward real change!

Finding healthy escapes for teens is crucial. There are plenty of rock-style Christian music artists out there. Perhaps you can help research some artists you think your teens may like. Worship, particularly music, is a great way to connect with God. Worship can help you reset your focus. Worship can put us into a state of gratitude instead of depression or frustration. Worship can cut through the dark in a lonely soul and even bring change to teens living the darkest lives.

> *Therefore, I urge you, brothers and sisters, in view of God's mercy, to offer your bodies as a living sacrifice, holy and pleasing to God—this is your true and proper worship. Do not conform to the pattern of this world, but be transformed by the renewing of your mind. Then you will be able to test and approve what God's will is—his good, pleasing and perfect will.*
>
> **Romans 12:1–2**

Dear Lord, worshiping You brings out the greatest joy. Thank You for music that can breathe life into our souls. I pray that we can all worship You in our everyday circumstances. I pray everyone reading this will find the gratitude that comes out of worship to You. I pray that our teens will hear something that will speak of You to their soul. Thank You for Your beautiful ways and sounds. Amen.

QUESTIONS FOR REFLECTION AND PERSONAL WORK

1.) Do I listen to music that would glorify God?

_____

_____

_____

_____

_____

_____

2.) Do I know what my teen is listening to?

_____

_____

_____

_____

_____

_____

3.) Can I put music on in my house that speaks of life and love?

_____

_____

_____

4.) Would I consider taking my teen to a Christian concert?

5.) What do I think my teen is worshiping?

CHAPTER 34:

THE ULTIMATE RELATIONSHIP

Does the road to living victoriously seem like a long one? Well, it will be. There is a lot to learn and a lot of work to be done to change one's mental health; it certainly does not happen overnight. Our relationship with Jesus can take years to build, especially to change your life. I've known Jesus as my Savior since that wonderful night as a sixteen-year-old at a youth function, but I didn't know until many years later that I could have a relationship with Him.

So how do you have a relationship with someone you can't see, touch, or smell? How do you have a relationship with the Almighty God? For one, we have the Bible (God's Word) for God to reveal all that He desires for us. The more we get to know God's Word, the more we get to know Him! God's Word is truth and light. God's Word is good, not evil. God's Word is full of hope and love. God's Word is powerful and full of grace. If you are not sure, read the Bible and I guarantee that God will take care of the rest.

Second, we have prayer. This is how we speak to God. When we are honest and lift our worries to God, He is there! He hears and answers prayers of *"those who earnestly seek him."* God knows what is on our hearts and minds, but God wants us to speak it!

We also have quietness and meditation and reflection. Being still and quiet and meditating on His Word and greatness is how God speaks to us! There will be much revealed to us when we are still and concentrate. Sometimes God can speak to us through music, nature, water, and even exercise when we concentrate on His goodness.

When we start our dialogue of praying and speaking to God, and we hear back, this is when we will start to see our purpose like never before. We begin to identify ourselves with eternal worth rather than external possessions or professions. There is no better way to live than to live purposefully. You will have *"peace that surpasses all understanding."* I know as parents we also want this for our children!

Dear Lord, I pray that all who are reading this will discover the joy and peace that comes from having a relationship with You. I know You want that too. Help us to understand that it is not some task to complete or a box to check off, but rather a lifestyle that we can have when we plug into the Creator of our universe. How cool is that?

I pray that the strongholds that control us can be broken with this relationship. You are the Wonderful Counselor, the Great I Am. Thank You for your promise of eternity with You. May we all find that ultimate location someday with the ultimate relationship with You. Amen.

QUESTIONS FOR REFLECTION AND PERSONAL WORK

1.) Would I like this relationship with God?

_____

_____

_____

_____

_____

_____

_____

2.) What is stopping me from trying to get to know God?

_____

_____

_____

_____

_____

_____

_____

3.) What do I think of the eternal consequences if I don't try?

_____

_____

_____

THE ULTIMATE RELATIONSHIP

4.) Would it be worth a try knowing them? (Heaven or Hell?)

5.) Do I think God can reveal something new to me?

CHAPTER 35:

THE FINAL DESTINATION

What is our final destination? If our life priorities are working, or waiting to retire, we have missed the purpose. If we are only working and waiting for that promotion, we have missed the purpose. If we are only concerned about getting married, we have missed the purpose. If we are only waiting and trying to have kids, we have missed the purpose. These are all wonderful things, but if we believe in salvation, if we really believe in the reality of Heaven, then isn't that the way we should live? Isn't that what we should be working towards? To live like we were dying soon!

Imagine how purposeful and intentional we would be with our lives and our relationships. If our actions are not faith-filled and we are not living for God, then we have missed the magnitude of living with God in Heaven.

God has promised that Heaven will be a place of purity, joy, compassion, generosity, and harmony among all people who live and trust in Christ. That sure doesn't sound like our world at all, does it? We work and look forward to a vacation, but boy, Heaven will be the ultimate vacation. If we embraced this destination, then our relationship with Christ would be a big deal! He is our ticket to Heaven, our final destination!

For some of us that have lost loved ones, this is great news. We will get the chance to continue our relationship in the most glorious setting with the ones that we have loved and lost. Only someone as big as God could come up with such a plan! For us parents that have children that seem so distant from God, don't give up! Continue to pray in faith. God is working even when we don't see it.

Dear Lord, thank You that we have so much to look forward to. Thank You that these 50–100 years here on earth will be like a blink compared to eternity with You. Thank You for the promise of no more suffering, no more sickness, and no more pain. Only you, the Designer and Creator of this amazing world, could come up with such a grand-slam ending. Help us keep our eyes on the prize. Thank You that You "will repay each person according to what they have done. To those who by persistence in doing good seek glory, honor and immortality, he will give eternal life" (Romans 2:6–7).

QUESTIONS FOR REFLECTION AND PERSONAL WORK

1.) How would my relationship change with Christ if I knew I would have eternal life?

_____

_____

_____

_____

_____

_____

_____

2.) How can I share this good news with others?

_____

_____

_____

_____

_____

_____

3.) If my family is far from God, am I willing to help challenge them? How can I prepare for this?

_____

_____

_____

_____

_____

_____

_____

4.) Do I believe that God works for the good for those that believe in Him?

_____

_____

_____

_____

_____

5.) How can I realign my priorities?

_____

_____

_____

_____

_____

_____

6.) I will commit to memorizing my favorite verse.

_____

_____

_____

_____

_____

_____

_____

CONCLUSION

If we can embrace pain and serious adversity, it can help us become more like Christ. Otherwise, it can turn us into miserable human beings. Oftentimes, we try to parent our teen according to what we think is best, and yet our own lives are a complete mess. It is not selfish to work on yourself. When you are living for God in all areas of your life, it will help spill over to your teen. With God's help, prayer, and a changed attitude, we can use our difficulties and pain to glorify God. Keeping a heart of gratitude, even for the small things, such as a hot meal or a shower, can keep us in the mindset we need for success. Be positively aggressive! Stay focused so you can stay motivated. Practicing gratefulness in front of your teens is important, especially when your family is going through tough times.

Use the beautiful things around you, such as nature and music, to help you. Our minds will want to wander towards self-pity. Stay self-controlled with your thoughts. Gratefulness will always put us in a different mindset and give us peace. Peace is the only thing that can settle our hearts and minds.

Shift your thoughts and efforts onto others. I know this is not what the world tells us, but maybe that's why we have so many people living in anxiety and stress and with miserable lives. The world tells us to look out for ourselves, *do you, be you, do what makes you happy,* and yet those things do not give us peace. These ideas of *"self"* are thrown at our teenagers from social media, school, or you name it. That message will constantly be ringing in their ears. These are things we need to have conversations about with our children. They can be emotionally intelligent, depending on how we interact with them and what we expect. The only time I've ever seen *"do you"* make sense is during a workout.

Community may be the first area I would work on. Teens feel the need and often seek acceptance and belonging from others who will never give them that. Perhaps we can have an influence on this by intentionally setting up a mentor and youth group. Otherwise, that attention could come from unwanted sources. Establishing a mentor that teens can talk to outside of the home is so important. Helping them become a master at some kind of skill will help them feel accomplished, even if they are failing at other things. The need to help others and be generous is extremely important to their emotional health and growth. Hopefully, you have now been able to better identify an at-risk teen.

Serious reflection on God's Word and truth is the key to answered prayer and successful living. As David said, *"Oh, how I love your law! I meditate on it all day long"* (Psalm 119:97). With all that being said:

> *Love your God with all your heart and all your soul and with all your strength. These*

commandments that I give you today are to be upon your hearts. Impress them on your children. Talk about them when you sit at home and when you walk along the road, when you lie down and when you get up. Tie them as symbols on your hands and bind them on your foreheads. Write them on the doorframes of your houses and on your gates.

Deuteronomy 6:5–9

When you start feeling strong and secure in your faith and trust in God, it will help you to start helping your teen and your relationship. As I've stated in previous chapters, find a support system for your teen: A mentor, a therapist, a youth pastor, and if you are having an instinct that your situation is becoming dangerous, please seek help immediately. There are many programs such as Teen Challenge that are amazing rehabilitation centers.

Dear Lord, I pray right now that all who have read this can find peace in their families. Help them to find the most amazing peace in the middle of the direst circumstances. Reveal in them Your will, so they may help others in a way that is perfectly designed for them. I pray that their purpose will be known.

I pray that this may touch someone so deeply that they are moved to do something they thought was impossible. Lord, thank You for giving us that hope. I pray that their changes will be so big that it spills over to their children and the rest of their family. Thank You for giving us the will to continue for Your sake, even when we feel we have nothing left to give, or nothing left to live for. You really are the "Great I am, and the Prince of Peace." Amen!

Printed in the USA
CPSIA information can be obtained
at www.ICGtesting.com
CBHW071923160724
11691CB00005B/126